William Shakespeare's

EDUCATE.IE
SHAKESPEARE
SERIES

Catherine O'Donovan

educate.ie

Contents

Introduction

What do you already know about the play *Romeo and Juliet*?

Overview of the Play – Mapping the Plot

As you progress through the play, you will write a phrase to remind you about the main action in each scene.

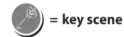 = key scene

	SCENE 1	SCENE 2	SCENE 3
ACT 1			
ACT 2		SCENE 2 (key scene)	
ACT 3	SCENE 1 (key scene)		
ACT 4			SCENE 3 (key scene)
ACT 5			SCENE 3 (key scene)

SCENE 4	SCENE 5
SCENE 4	SCENE 5	SCENE 6
SCENE 4	SCENE 5
SCENE 4	SCENE 5

Who's Who?

Pair Activity

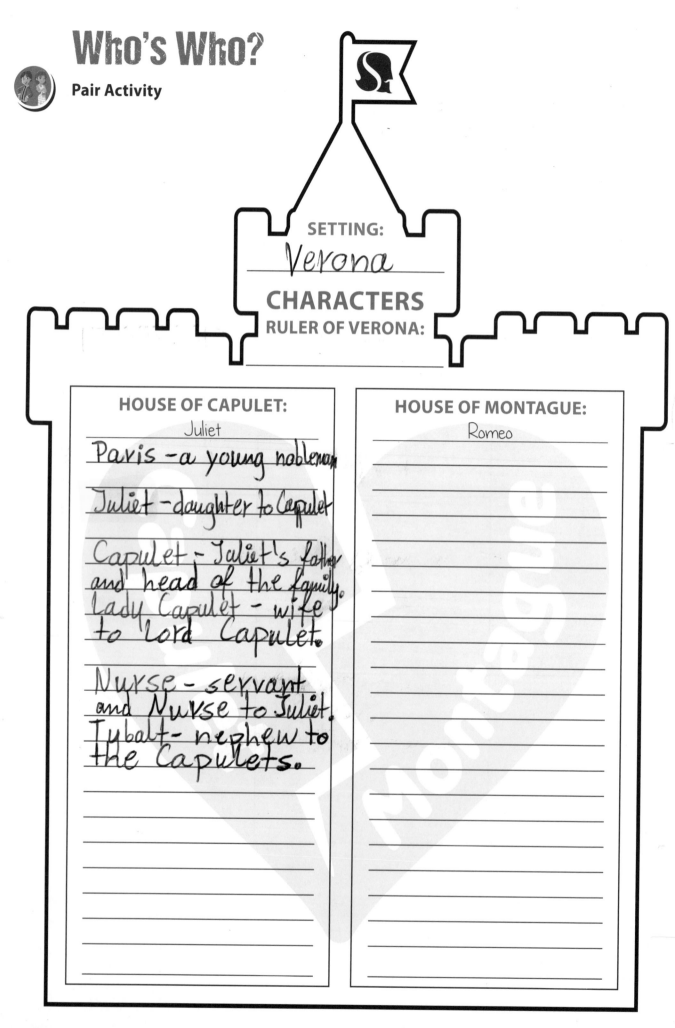

SETTING:

Verona

CHARACTERS

RULER OF VERONA:

HOUSE OF CAPULET:	HOUSE OF MONTAGUE:
Juliet	Romeo

HOUSE OF CAPULET:

Juliet

Paris - a young nobleman

Juliet - daughter to Capulet

Capulet - Juliet's father and head of the family.

Lady Capulet - wife to Lord Capulet.

Nurse - servant and Nurse to Juliet.

Tybalt - nephew to the Capulets.

HOUSE OF MONTAGUE:

Romeo

ACT 1, PROLOGUE

A. EXPLORING

Pair Activity

(a) With your partner, summarise the prologue. Use the boxes below to help you. Draw an image or a symbol to accompany your text.

First quatrain (lines 1–4):

In the first quatrain, we learn that the play is set in Verona and that an ancient feud between two noble families has been reignited (has started again)…

_____

_____

_____

_____

_____

_____

An image that stands out:

Second quatrain (lines 5–8):

The second quatrain tells us that…

_____

_____

_____

_____

An image that stands out:

Third quatrain (lines 9–12):

In the third quatrain, we learn that…

_____

_____

_____

_____

An image that stands out:

ACT 1, PROLOGUE

Couplet (lines 13–14):

> Finally,
>
> _____
>
> _____
>
> _____
>
> _____

An image that stands out:

(b) From the points you have written, what do you think the **main issues** will be in the play?

The main issue is love from Romeo to Juliet. They parents don't want them together because their families have conflict.

ACT 1, SCENE 1

B. EXPLORING

Romeo's Language – Metaphors

Read the following extract from **Act 1, Scene 1** (lines 183–187), in which Romeo outlines his opinion on love:

> Love is a smoke made with the fume of sighs,
> Being purged, a fire sparkling in lovers' eyes,
> Being vexed, a sea nourished with lovers' tears.
> What is it else? A madness most discreet,
> A choking gall and a preserving sweet.

(a) To what things does Romeo compare love in the extract above?

(b) Is his view of love positive or negative? Explain your answer.

(c) Write a short poem that includes as many **metaphors** as you can think of, starting with: '**Love is…**'

C. REFLECTING

2. My Reflection on Act 1, Scene 1

Write a paragraph outlining your **response to the events** in this scene. In your paragraph, you might mention the following:

- Something that you found **interesting/dramatic/exciting**
- Your first impression of the **characters**
- Something that might have **confused** you or that you are wondering about.

3. Considering Key Themes

(a) In your opinion, where is the **conflict** most evident in this scene?

_____

_____

_____

_____

_____

_____

_____

_____

_____

_____

_____

_____

(b) What do we learn about the **theme of love** in this scene?

_____

_____

_____

_____

_____

_____

_____

_____

_____

_____

_____

4. Key Quotes

Quote:	Speaker:	My interpretation:	Why I think it is important:
I do but keep the peace. Put up thy sword, *Or manage it to part these men with me.* (lines 61–62)	Benvolio	He doesn't want to fight, but wants to stop the fight.	This quote shows that Benvolio is a peacemaker, in contrast to Tybalt, who is a troublemaker.
What, drawn and talk of peace? I hate the word *As I hate hell, all Montagues, and thee.* (lines 63–64)			
If ever you disturb our streets again *Your lives shall pay the forfeit of the peace.* (lines 89–90)			
Tut, I have lost myself. I am not here. *This is not Romeo; he's some other where.* (lines 190–191)			

ACT 1, SCENE 2

C. REFLECTING

My Reflection on Act 1, Scene 2

(a) Write three points to recap on what happened in this scene.

Point one:

_____

_____

_____

_____

Point two:

_____

_____

_____

_____

Point three:

_____

_____

_____

_____

(b) Something I found surprising about this scene:

| |
| |

(c) One memorable quote from this scene, and what I think it might mean:

Quote:	My interpretation:

ACT 1, SCENE 3

B. EXPLORING

Imagery of Paris

(a) What do you think Lady Capulet means by the following lines?

This precious book of love, this unbound lover,
To beautify him, only lacks a cover. (lines 88–89)

_____

_____

_____

_____

_____

_____

(b) What other **images** are used to describe Paris in this scene? Find **two** more examples and write them down.

Example one:

_____

_____

_____

Example two:

_____

_____

_____

(c) What **impression** of Paris do these images give you?

_____

_____

_____

_____

_____

_____

ACT 1, SCENE 4

B. ORAL LANGUAGE

Pair Activity

2. Imagery: Drawing Queen Mab

- Draw a picture to illustrate your impressions of Queen Mab.
- Look back over lines 55–96 of the scene help you.
- **Use quotes to label your picture**, for example: 'Her chariot [carriage] is an empty hazelnut' (line 68).

C. EXPLORING

Research: Cupid, God of Love

Cupid, the god of love in Roman mythology, is referred to frequently in the play. In **Act 1, Scene 1**, Romeo mentions Cupid when discussing Rosaline. Can you remember what he says about him? (Refer to lines 164–165 and lines 201–202 in particular.)

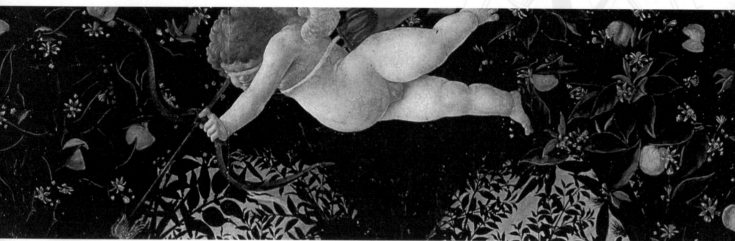

Pair Activity

(a) With your partner, look up facts about Cupid and fill in the grid below.

Profile: Cupid

Mother	
Father	
Characteristics/ distinguishing features	
How is Cupid depicted (shown) in art, music and literature?	
Is Cupid generally seen as a positive or negative influence?	

(b) Why do you think Shakespeare refers to Cupid so often in the play?

_____

_____

_____

_____

_____

ACT 1, SCENE 5

The Capulet feast

B. ORAL LANGUAGE

Pair Activity

In **Romeo and Juliet's shared sonnet**, Romeo uses a lot of **religious imagery**. He imagines himself as a pilgrim going to worship at the holy shrine of Juliet.

> **ROMEO**
>
> If I profane with my unworthiest hand
> This holy shrine, the gentle sin is this:
> My lips, two blushing pilgrims, ready stand
> To smooth that rough touch with a tender kiss.
>
> **JULIET**
>
> Good pilgrim, you do wrong your hand too much,
> Which mannerly devotion shows in this.
> For saints have hands that pilgrims' hands do touch,
> And palm to palm is holy palmers' kiss.
>
> **ROMEO**
>
> Have not saints lips, and holy palmers, too?
>
> **JULIET**
>
> Ay, pilgrim, lips that they must use in prayer.
>
> **ROMEO**
>
> O then, dear saint, let lips do what hands do:
> They pray, grant thou, lest faith turn to despair.
>
> **JULIET**
>
> Saints do not move, though grant for prayers' sake.
>
> **ROMEO**
>
> Then move not, while my prayers' effect I take.

(a) With your partner, **read** the extract above. One person should read Romeo's lines and the other should read Juliet's. Read it again, swapping the roles.

(b) With your partner, <u>underline</u> all of the words in the extract that are **religious or that might have religious associations**. Write down some examples in the grid below:

(c) Discuss why you think Romeo uses **religious language** here. Write down one point.

_____

_____

_____

_____

_____

_____

_____

(d) Discuss how you think **Romeo's character** has changed in this scene. Write down one point.

_____

_____

_____

_____

_____

_____

_____

_____

C. REFLECTING

1. My Reflection on Act 1, Scene 5 – a Key Scene

(a) Complete the following grid:

Who are the main characters?	
What happens?	
Where is the scene set?	
Why do the characters act the way they do?	
Something I found memorable/ surprising:	
Something that confused me:	
A question I have in mind after reading this scene:	

(b) Write a paragraph outlining your **response to the events** in this scene. In your paragraph, you might mention the following:

- Something that you found **interesting/dramatic/exciting**
- Your first impression of the **characters**
- Something that might have **confused** you or that you are wondering about.

_____

_____

_____

_____

_____

_____

_____

_____

_____

_____

_____

_____

_____

_____

_____

_____

_____

_____

_____

_____

_____

_____

_____

_____

_____

_____

ACT 1, SCENE 5

2. Key Quotes

Complete the following grid and learn these key quotes:

Quote:	Speaker:	My interpretation:
Did my heart love till now? Forswear it, sight, *For I ne'er saw true beauty till this night.* (lines 50–51)		
I will withdraw, but this intrusion shall *Now seeming sweet convert to bitterest gall.* (lines 91–92)		
My only love sprung from my only hate! *Too early seen unknown, and known too late!* *Prodigious birth of love it is to me* *That I must love a loathèd enemy.* (lines 138–141)		

D. CREATING

Writing a Magazine Article

You are a reporter for the popular, glitzy Veronese magazine, *Good Morrow!* You have been asked to report on the Capulet feast.

Capulet Feast Guest List

Signior Martino and his wife and daughters. County Anselme and his beauteous sisters. The lady Widow of Vitruvio. Signior Placentio and his lovely nieces. Mercutio and his brother Valentine. Mine uncle Capulet, his wife and daughters. My fair niece Rosaline and Livia. Signior Valentio and his cousin Tybalt. Lucio and the lively Helena.

(Romeo, Act 1, Scene 2, lines 66–72)

Guidelines

Using the guest list for the Capulet feast as a guide, find small photographs of the guests and attach them to the layout on page 23. Write their names underneath the photographs. (You could also draw pictures in the spaces provided.)

Write a **brief article** outlining the events of the night. You might have noticed Capulet becoming angry with Tybalt, or a mysterious stranger talking to Juliet. Perhaps you spoke to/interviewed one or more of the guests or servants. You may handwrite your article in the layout, or type it.

Good Morrow! Exclusive

ACT 2, PROLOGUE 🌹

A. ORAL LANGUAGE

Reading and Summarising the Prologue

Pair Activity

(a) With your partner, take turns reading the prologue. Listen closely to your partner's reading without looking at the text. Listen out for any **positive** *or* **negative** words or phrases and list them in the grid below. Then swap roles.

Positive words	Negative words
young affection	death-bed

(b) Compare your list of words with that of your partner. In your opinion, is the prologue more positive or negative overall?

_____

(c) With your partner, summarise the prologue. Use the boxes below to help you. Pick out one quote to accompany each quatrain and the couplet. (This may be just one or two words.)

First quatrain (lines 1–4):

One quote that stands out:

In the first quatrain, we learn that…	

Second quatrain (lines 5–8):

The second quatrain tells us that…

_____

_____

_____

_____

_____

One quote that stands out:

Third quatrain (lines 9–12):

In the third quatrain, we learn that…

_____

_____

_____

_____

_____

One quote that stands out:

Couplet (lines 13–14):

Finally,

_____

_____

_____

_____

_____

One quote that stands out:

(d) Summarise the prologue in one sentence.

_____

_____

_____

_____

# ACT 2, SCENE 2

The Balcony Scene

B. ORAL LANGUAGE

1. Romeo's Soliloquy

Pair Activity

(a) Read Romeo's soliloquy (lines 2–25) with your partner, taking turns at each punctuation mark. Next, <u>underline</u> any word associated with **brightness** or **light**. Read the soliloquy a second time together, emphasising (or exaggerating) the words that you have underlined.

Juliet's eyes are brighter than the brightest stars in heaven.

(b) Romeo attempts to describe how bright and beautiful Juliet's eyes are by comparing them to the brightest stars in heaven (the sky). His comparison is an example of **hyperbole** – exaggeration. This is a complicated idea, so let's break it down. Write the appropriate lines from Romeo's soliloquy to match each point below:

Point one: The stars are leaving their orbit in the sky and have asked Juliet's eyes to take their place while they are gone.

_____
_____
_____
_____

Point two: Juliet's eyes will replace these bright stars in the sky.

_____
_____
_____

Point three: The stars will replace Juliet's eyes.

_____
_____
_____

Point four: The results of this exchange or swap are:

• Juliet's bright cheek will outshine those stars.

_____
_____
_____

• Juliet's eyes, which have replaced the stars in the sky, will shine so brightly that the birds will think it is not night and sing as if it were day-time.

_____
_____
_____

C. EXPLORING

1. Language Devices in the Balcony Scene

Look at the quotes below and say whether each one uses a **metaphor**, a **simile**, or an example of **personification**. Next, explain the **effect** of the language device used in each quote.

Quote:	Device:	Effect of this device:
It is the east, and Juliet is the sun! (line 3)	metaphor	Romeo is comparing Juliet to the sun. He is saying that Juliet is radiant and beautiful. This creates a bright, positive image.
Arise, fair sun, and kill the envious moon, *Who is already sick and pale with grief* (lines 4–5)		
O, speak again, bright angel (line 26)		
My ears have yet not drunk a hundred words *Of thy tongue's uttering* (lines 58–59)		
This bud of love, by summer's ripening breath, *May prove a beauteous flower when next we meet.* (lines 121–122)		
My bounty is as boundless as the sea, *My love as deep.* (lines 133–134)		
Love goes toward love, as schoolboys from their books (line 156)		
How silver-sweet sound lovers' tongues by night, *Like softest music to attending ears!* (lines 165–166)		

2. The Language of Love in the Balcony Scene

Pair Activity

(a) Read the quotes from **Act 2, Scene 2** below. Without looking at the textbook, tick the appropriate box to indicate whether you think the speaker is Romeo or Juliet. When you have finished, compare your answers with those of your partner.

Quote:	Speaker:	
	Romeo	Juliet
With love's light wings did I o'er-perch these walls; *For stony limits cannot hold love out* (lines 66–67)		
I am no pilot, yet wert thou as far *As that vast shore washed with the farthest sea,* *I would adventure for such merchandise.* (lines 82–84)		
Dost thou love me? I know thou wilt say 'Ay', *And I will take thy word.* (lines 90–91)		
But trust me, gentleman, I'll prove more true *Than those that have more cunning to be strange.* (lines 100–101)		
Lady, by yonder blessèd moon I vow *That tips with silver all these fruit-tree tops* (lines 107–108)		
O swear not by the moon, th'inconstant moon, *That monthly changes in her circled orb,* *Lest that thy love prove likewise variable.* (lines 109–111)		
Although I joy in thee, *I have no joy of this contract tonight.* *It is too rash, too unadvised, too sudden* (lines 116–118)		
My bounty is as boundless as the sea, *My love as deep. The more I give to thee,* *The more I have, for both are infinite.* (lines 133–135)		
If that thy bent of love be honourable, *Thy purpose marriage, send me word tomorrow,* *By one that I'll procure to come to thee* (lines 143–145)		

ACT 2, SCENE 2

(b) Look back over the quotes on page 29 and write a paragraph comparing Romeo and Juliet's views on love. For example, one might suggest that Romeo is more spontaneous and impulsive, whereas Juliet is more cautious and realistic. What do you think?

_____
_____
_____
_____
_____
_____
_____
_____
_____
_____
_____
_____
_____
_____
_____
_____
_____
_____
_____
_____
_____
_____
_____
_____
_____
_____
_____
_____
_____
_____
_____
_____

 D. REFLECTING

1. My Reflection on Act 2, Scene 2 – a Key Scene

(a) Complete the following grid:

Who are the main characters?	
What happens?	
Where is the scene set?	
Why do the characters act the way they do?	
Something I found memorable/ surprising:	
Something that confused me:	
A question I have in mind after reading this scene:	

ACT 2, SCENE 2

(b) Write a paragraph outlining your **response to the events** in this scene. In your paragraph, you might mention the following:

- Something that you found **interesting/dramatic/exciting**
- Your first impression of the **characters**
- Something that might have **confused** you or that you are wondering about.

_____

_____

_____

_____

_____

_____

_____

_____

_____

_____

_____

_____

_____

_____

_____

_____

_____

_____

_____

_____

_____

_____

_____

_____

_____

_____

_____

_____

E. PROJECT
Guidelines for Your Group Project

1. Setting and Type of Stage

- **When** and **where** would your production be set? Would it be classical or modern?
- What type of stage would you use? (See below for ideas.)
- Think about the set design.
- Think about props (all objects other than furniture and costumes that you would use in the scene).

2. Visual and Aural Effects

What effects would you use to bring the scene to life? Think about the following:

- Lighting
- Costume
- Music
- Sound effects.

3. Characters

How would you direct the characters in this scene? Think about the following:

- Positioning of the characters on stage
- Movement
- Advice that you would give to the actors about their lines
- Facial expressions.

You may present the project as a **poster, computer presentation, booklet, video, model,** or a **combination** of any of these.

Types of Stage

Take a look at some of the different types of stage below, which might help you with your project:

1. Elizabethan Open-air Theatre

Shakespeare's Globe Theatre was an example of an Elizabethan open-air theatre. It was first built in Southwark, London in 1599. A reconstruction of the original theatre was opened in 1997 and remains a popular tourist attraction today.

Globe Theatre

2. Proscenium Arch Stage

This is the most common type of stage. It is also known as a 'picture frame theatre'. The audience faces the stage on one side. Sometimes the stage can jut out a little, and this is known as the 'apron'.

3. Theatre in the Round

Theatre in the round is where the stage is in the centre of the theatre and the audience surrounds the stage. This type of stage is also known as an arena stage. The stage does not have to be round. It may be square, like a boxing ring arena.

4. Thrust Stage

A thrust stage is a stage that is surrounded by the audience on three sides. It is more intimate than the proscenium stage and has the added benefit of a backstage area – something that an arena stage does not have.

5. Found Space Theatre

Found or created space theatres are very modern. These are spaces that are not purpose-built for theatre. They are often old warehouses or disused buildings.

Costume

Below are sketches of costumes for a production of *Romeo and Juliet*. What is your opinion of these designs?

Juliet's costume for the Capulet Feast Scene

Juliet's costume for the Balcony Scene

Positioning of Characters on Stage

The positioning of characters on stage is very important. The space that characters occupy on stage tells the audience how important they are in a scene. The diagram below is used to help direct the position of characters on a typical proscenium stage. The directions are from the actor's viewpoint, not the audience's. So, for example, a character entering stage right will be on the audience's left. Upstage is the back of the stage from the audience's viewpoint. Downstage is the front of the stage from the audience's viewpoint.

upstage right	upstage	upstage left
centre right	centre stage	centre left
downstage right	downstage	downstage left

Audience

'Parting is such sweet sorrow
That I shall say good night till it be morrow.'
(Juliet, Act 2, Scene 2, lines 184–185)

Producing and Presenting a Scene

Group Activity

Use the grid below to start **planning your project**.

Setting and Type of Stage	
When and where would your production be set? What type of stage would you use? Set design: Props:	
Visual and Aural Effects	
What effects would you use to bring the scene to life? Lighting: Costume: Music: Sound effects:	
Format of the Presentation	
You may present the project as a poster, computer presentation, booklet, video, model, or a combination of any of these. What format do you have in mind? What will your role be?	

My Reflection on the Project

When you have finished presenting your project, write a **reflection** on your involvement in the project. Mention the following:

• Your role in the project work
• The key things you learned from doing this project
• Something that you might have done differently.

_____

_____

_____

_____

_____

_____

_____

_____

_____

_____

_____

_____

_____

_____

_____

_____

_____

_____

_____

_____

_____

_____

_____

_____

My Reflection on the Project (continued)

_____
_____
_____
_____
_____
_____
_____
_____
_____
_____
_____
_____
_____
_____
_____
_____
_____
_____
_____
_____
_____
_____
_____
_____
_____
_____
_____
_____
_____
_____
_____
_____

ACT 2, SCENE 3

B. EXPLORING

Antithesis and Personification in Friar Laurence's Language

Pair Activity

(a) Friar Laurence's words are full of **opposites** (antithesis), reminding us that this play is all about **conflict**. Look back over lines 1–35 of Act 2, Scene 3 and fill in the grid below. (**Hints**: Youth versus old age, good versus evil, light versus dark, life versus death, etc.)

Opposites:	Examples:
Youth v. old age	'old man's eye' v. 'youth with unstuffed brain'
Good v. evil	

(b) Can you find an example of **personification** in this scene? What effect does it have? Write your answers in the grid below.

Example of personification:	Effect of personification:

C. REFLECTING

2. Key Quotes

Look at the key quotes from **Act 2, Scene 3** in the grid below and write what you think each one might mean in the box beside it.

Quote:	My interpretation:
Two such opposèd kings encamp them still *In man as well as herbs – grace and rude will* (Friar Laurence, lines 27–28)	
I have been feasting with mine enemy (Romeo, line 49)	
For this alliance may so happy prove, *To turn your households' rancour to pure love.* (Friar Laurence, lines 91–92)	
Wisely and slow. They stumble that run fast. (Friar Laurence, line 94)	

ACT 2, SCENE 4

B. EXPLORING

1. Tybalt's Letter to Romeo

2. Research: Classical Lovers

(a) Research the tragic women whom Mercutio mentions in his speech (lines 39–41). For each, find out **who she was,** who her **partner** was and **what happened** to her. Write your findings in the grid below.

Who she was:	Her partner:	What happened to her:
Dido was…		
Cleopatra		
Helen		
Hero		
Thisbe		

(b) Why do you think Shakespeare included these classical references in Mercutio's speech?

_____

_____

_____

(c) Now that you know more about these tragic women, what kind of atmosphere does mentioning them help to create?

_____

_____

ACT 2, SCENE 5

B. CREATING

Juliet's Diary

Juliet's Diary (continued)

ACT 3, SCENE 1

The Fight Scene

B. EXPLORING

1. Who Killed Whom?

- Using Benvolio's summary of events (lines 150–173) as a guide, draw the **eight main stages** of the scene in the boxes below and on the next page. Don't worry if you are not a skilled artist – stick figures are acceptable, and you could use a different colour for each character.

- Write a **sentence or quote** below each picture to explain what happens in this part of the scene.

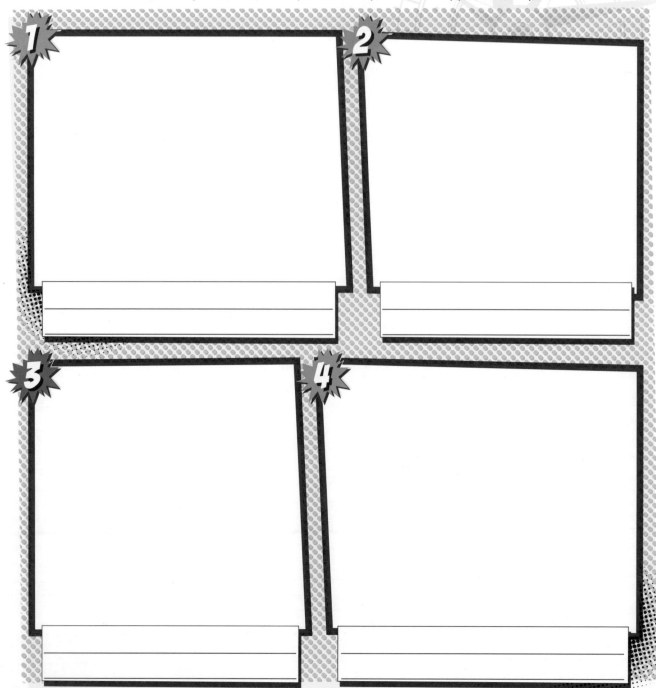

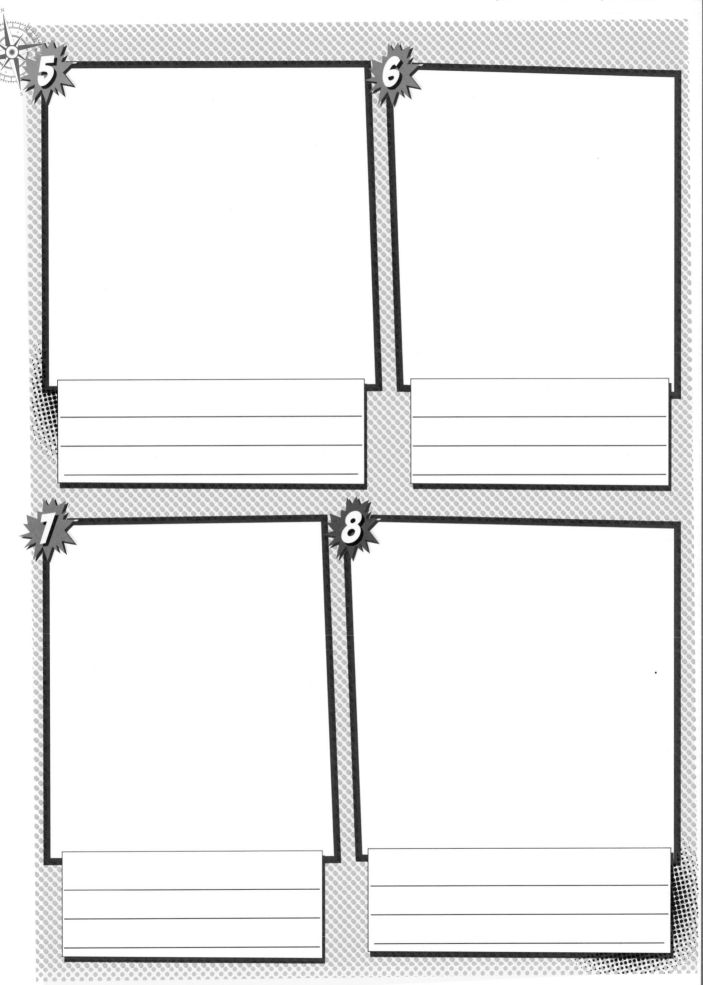

2. Characters

Pair Activity

What part did each of the characters play in this scene? Fill in the grid below.

Character:	What he did in this scene:	An adjective to describe this character:	A key quote from him in this scene:
Benvolio			
Mercutio			
Romeo			
Tybalt			

C. CREATING

Write a front-page news story reporting on the events that took place in this scene.

The Verona Times

YOUR DAILY NEWSPAPER

The *Verona Times* (continued)

D. REFLECTING

1. My Reflection on Act 3, Scene 1 – a Key Scene

Complete the following grid:

Who are the main characters?	
What happens?	
Where is the scene set?	
Why do the characters act the way they do?	
Something I found memorable/ surprising:	
Something that confused me:	
A question I have in mind after reading this scene:	

2. Key Quotes

Write out three quotes that you think are important in Act 3, Scene 1 and say what you think they might mean.

Quote:	My interpretation:

ACT 3, SCENE 2

B. EXPLORING

Juliet's Language

(a) Look again at Juliet's immediate response to the news that Romeo has killed her cousin, Tybalt (lines 73–85). Can you find three more examples of an **oxymoron** in her speech? Write them in the grid below and draw a picture to illustrate each one.

Example of oxymoron:	Picture:
'fiend angelical' (line 75)	

(b) Why do you think Juliet uses so many **oxymorons** in her language in this particular part of the scene?

D. REFLECTING

Juliet's Character

Pair Activity

(a) Juliet experiences a range of conflicting emotions in this scene. With your partner, try to find examples of the different emotions that she feels. Read back over the scene and complete the following grid:

Emotion:	Quote:	My interpretation:
Excitement	*So tedious is this day* *As is the night before some festival* *To an impatient child that hath new robes* *And may not wear them.* (lines 28–31)	I think this quote shows that Juliet is excited and impatient, as she compares herself to a child who has new clothes and wants to wear them immediately.

(b) Using the information above as a guide, turn to **page 92** of the **Character File** section and write about how Juliet comes across in this scene.

ACT 3, SCENE 3

B. ORAL LANGUAGE

Performing Friar Laurence's Speech to Romeo

Group Activity

Write the summary of each section of Friar Laurence's speech to Romeo in the grid below.

Speech section:	Summary of Friar Laurence's main points to Romeo:
One Friar Laurence rebukes Romeo for not seeing how fortunate he is (lines 108–134).	He said that he don't need to cry, because he is so intelligent and good.
Two Friar Laurence outlines all of the things for which Romeo should be grateful (lines 135–145).	He said to Romeo that he need to be grateful, because he killed Tybalt.
Three Friar Laurence outlines his plan to help Romeo (lines 146–158).	He ~~tells~~ said that he need to meet with Juliet.

C. EXPLORING

Romeo's Language – Hyperbole

Find two examples of **hyperbole** (exaggeration) in Romeo's language in this scene. State what you think is the effect of hyberbole in each of these examples.

Example of hyperbole:	Effect of hyperbole:
1.	
2.	

ACT 3, SCENE 5

B. EXPLORING

1. Double Meanings in Juliet's Speech

Juliet's answers to her mother in this scene are vague and full of double meanings. Read the quotes from Juliet below and outline the two possible interpretations for each one.

Quote:	What Juliet's mother thinks she means:	What Juliet actually means:
God pardon him – I do, with all my heart. *And yet no man like he doth grieve my heart.* (lines 82–83)		
Indeed, I never shall be satisfied *With Romeo, till I behold him – dead –* *Is my poor heart so for a kinsman vexed.* (lines 93–95)		
O, how my heart abhors *To hear him named, and cannot come to him* *To wreak the love I bore my cousin Tybalt* *Upon his body that hath slaughtered him!* (lines 99–102)		

2. Capulet's Description of Juliet as a Ship in a Storm

(a) Capulet describes Juliet in her upset state as a ship at sea during a storm – 'tempest-tossèd' (line 137). Read back over lines 129–137 and fill in the grid below.

	Quote:	My interpretation:
Juliet's eyes	'Do ebb and flow with tears.'	This quote tells us that Juliet's tears resemble the waves of the sea, which rise and fall.
Juliet's sighs		
Juliet's body		

(b) Considering the events that are unfolding in Juliet's life at this point in the play, do you think the image of her as **a ship in a storm** is appropriate? Explain your answer.

_____

_____

_____

_____

_____

_____

_____

_____

_____

_____

_____

_____

_____

ACT 3, SCENE 5

3. Capulet's Language

Pair Activity

(a) Look over Capulet's speech in lines 176–196. With your partner, paraphrase the main points that he makes to Juliet.

_____
_____
_____
_____
_____
_____
_____
_____
_____
_____
_____
_____
_____
_____
_____
_____
_____
_____

(b) List five examples of offensive things that Capulet says to Juliet.

In my own words, he says:	Quote:
1. MOST OFFENSIVE	
2.	
3.	
4.	
5. LEAST OFFENSIVE	

(c) My impression of Capulet in this scene:

_____
_____
_____

C. ORAL LANGUAGE

2. Imagery

Choose **two** important/memorable quotes from this scene and write and illustrate them below.

Quote:	My illustration:
1.	
2.	

D. REFLECTING

1. My Reflection on Act 3, Scene 5

List two things that you found **surprising** or that **stood out** to you in Act 3, Scene 5. Explain why you found them surprising or why they stood out to you.

_____

_____

_____

_____

_____

_____

_____

ACT 3, SCENE 5

E. CREATING

Writing a Prologue for Act 3

Planning:

- What **main idea** will you put in each of the three quatrains?
- What will your **conclusion** be for the **couplet** (the final two lines)?
- Use the grid below to help you.

Prologue for Act 3	Rhyming scheme:
	A
	B
	A
	B
	C
	D
	C
	D
	E
	F
	E
	F
	G
	G

ACT 4, SCENE 1

B. EXPLORING

Things Juliet Would Rather Do than Marry Paris

(a) Look over lines 77–88 from this scene and **list** all of the things that Juliet says she would rather do than marry Paris in the boxes below. Draw a picture (or find a picture) to illustrate each one. Look at the example below:

1. She would rather jump off the battlements of a tower.	
2. She would rather walk in places were thieves are.	
3. Chain her with roaring bears.	

4. Completely covered with dead men's ratt--ling bones, with stinking limbs, and yellow chapless skulls.	
5. Hide her nightly in a charnel house.	
6. Bid her lurk ~~she~~ where serpents are.	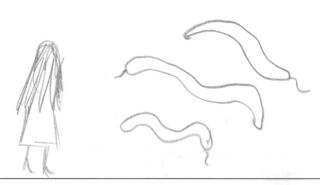

(b) What does all of this tell us about Juliet's **character**?

Juliet is stubborn and very confident. She rather die that marry Paris.

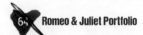

C. ORAL LANGUAGE

Friar Laurence's Plan

Pair Activity

(a) Look back over Friar Laurence's plan (lines 89–120) and write the key points of the plan in the grid below:

1. **Go home and agree to marry Paris.**
2.
3.
4.
5.
6.
7.

(b) Discuss: What do you think of Friar Laurence's plan? Write down two **positive aspects** and two **negative aspects** of his plan.

Positive aspect:	Negative aspect:
1.	1.
2.	2.

Junior Cycle English 65

 **ACT 4, SCENE 1**

(c) Do you think that this plan could work? What potential **problems** could there be?

(d) Can you think of an **alternative plan** or a way to improve on this one?

ACT 4, SCENE 3

The Potion Scene

B. EXPLORING

Juliet's Soliloquy

Pair Activity

With your partner, complete the following grid on Juliet's fears as she is about to take the potion. Describe each **fear** that she mentions and write the **appropriate quote**.

Juliet is afraid that:	Quote:
1. The potion will not work.	'What if this mixture do not work at all?' (line 21)
2.	
3.	
4.	

ACT 4, SCENE 5

A. EXPLORING

1. Reactions to the Discovery of Juliet's 'Death'

Pair Activity

(a) How does each character respond to the discovery of Juliet's 'death'? With your partner, look back over the scene and describe the characters' reactions. Use the grid below to help you.

Character:	Quote to sum up his/her reaction:	Description of his/her reaction:
The Nurse	"But one, poor one, one poor and loving child, but one thing to rejoice and solace in, and cruel death hath catched it from my sight!"	She mean that she want to wake up her from sleep & death.
Lady Capulet	"I must needs wake up. My lady! lady! lady! Alas alas! Help, help! My lady's dead!"	She mean that she get lovely child and she get comfort.
Capulet	"O child, O child, my soul and not my child! Dead art thou, alack, my child is dead, And with my child my joys are buried!"	He mean that his daughter is dead and he is so sad.
Paris	"Beguiled, divorced, wronged, spited, slain! Most detestable death, by thee beguiled."	She mean that she was cheated and killed.

(b) For which character do you have the most **sympathy** in this scene? Explain your answer.

_____
_____
_____
_____
_____
_____
_____
_____
_____
_____

2. Language Devices

Pair Activity

Look at the quotes below and say whether each one is an example of **simile**, **personification** or **repetition**. Next, briefly discuss the **effect** of each language device in this scene. For example, repeating a word (repetition) could emphasise it, while personification may create a clear or vivid image in the reader's mind.

Quote:	Device:	Effect:
O woe! O woeful, woeful, woeful day! Most lamentable day! (the Nurse, lines 49–50)		
Death lies on her like an untimely frost Upon the sweetest flower of all the field. (Capulet, lines 28–29)		
Death is my son-in-law, Death is my heir. My daughter he hath wedded. (Capulet, lines 38–39)		

ACT 5, SCENE 1 ✝

B. EXPLORING

Imagery of the Apothecary's Shop

Draw a cartoon/picture of the Apothecary in his shop. (Look back over lines 37–56.) Label your cartoon/picture using quotes from the scene. Also, include a speech bubble for Romeo and another for the Apothecary, each containing an **important quote** from this character in the scene.

ACT 5, SCENE 2 ✝

 ## A. CREATING

Friar Laurence's Letter to Romeo

ACT 5, SCENE 3 ✝

B. EXPLORING

1. Comparing Romeo and Paris as Love Rivals

(a) Compare the **actions** and **words** of Romeo and Paris in this scene. Use the grid below to help you.

	Paris	Romeo
His reason for being at the graveyard:		
His behaviour/ actions in this scene:		
His words:		

(b) How do you feel about Romeo and Paris at this point in the play? Explain your answer.

_____

_____

_____

_____

_____

_____

_____

_____

_____

_____

2. Language and Imagery

(a) Read back over Romeo's **soliloquy** (lines 87–120) and **paraphrase** the following questions that he asks in this speech:

Quote:	My interpretation:
Ah, dear Juliet, *Why art thou yet so fair?* (lines 101–102)	
Shall I believe *That unsubstantial Death is amorous,* *And that the lean abhorrèd monster keeps* *Thee here in dark to be his paramour?* (lines 102–105)	

(b) **Find** two examples of **personification** in this scene and comment on the **effect** of each one.

Example:	Effect:
1.	
2.	

(c) Find **two descriptions** of the tomb in this scene and discuss the **image** that is created by each one in your mind.

Description:	Image created:
1.	
2.	

C. CREATING

1. Romeo's Letter to his Father

2. Sketching the Scene

(a) Sketch your design of a **stage set** suitable for the final scene of *Romeo and Juliet*. Include **stage directions**.

(b) Write a **short piece** to accompany your design, indicating how the distinct parts of the scene could be played.

_____

(c) Pick out a few **important lines** from Paris, Romeo, Juliet, Friar Laurence and Prince Escalus, and say how you would expect the actors to deliver these lines.

_____

ACT 5, SCENE 3

E. ORAL LANGUAGE

1. Friar Laurence's Speech

Pair Activity

With your partner, summarise each section of Friar Laurence's speech in the grid below. Write only **one sentence** in each box.

	One-sentence summary:
Section 1 – lines 229–236:	
Section 2 – lines 237–246:	
Section 3 – lines 247–251:	
Section 4 – lines 252–259:	
Section 5 – lines 260–264:	
Section 6 – lines 265–269:	

Junior Cycle English 77

ACT 5, SCENE 3

2. Performing the Trial of Friar Laurence

Group Activity

Witness 1: The Nurse

Lawyers for Capulet/Montague families:	Lawyers for Friar Laurence:
Q.1	Q.1
Q.2	Q.2

Witness 2: Benvolio

Lawyers for Capulet/Montague families:	Lawyers for Friar Laurence:
Q.1	Q.1
Q.2	Q.2

Witness 3: Balthasar

Lawyers for Capulet/Montague families:	Lawyers for Friar Laurence:
Q.1	Q.1
Q.2	Q.2

Witness 4: Paris's Page

Lawyers for Capulet/Montague families:	Lawyers for Friar Laurence:
Q.1	Q.1
Q.2	Q.2

Closing statement from lawyers for Montague and Capulet families

Main points:

_____

_____

_____

_____

_____

_____

_____

_____

_____

Closing statement from lawyers for Friar Laurence

Main points:

_____

_____

_____

_____

_____

_____

_____

_____

Character File

This section of the portfolio will help you to keep track of the main characters in the play. Write down your response to the characters as you progress through the play. Use the list of useful adjectives on page 81 to help you.

Think about:

- What the character **does** in each key scene.
- The **adjectives** you would use to describe him/her.
- **Something that stands** out to you in a key scene.
- How the character **reacts to situations**.
- A significant **change** in the character.
- Something that **confuses or surprises you** about the character in a particular scene.
- How the character **interacts** with other characters, i.e. his/her **relationships** with others.
- What **other characters** say about the character.

CHARACTER FILE

Useful Adjectives

loving	courageous	diffident	quarrelsome
caring	inconsistent	capricious	practical
dutiful	reticent	unpredictable	unsupportive
obedient	timorous	treacherous	reassuring
faithful	deferential	disloyal	sympathetic
loyal	unsociable	misguided	empathetic
devoted	secretive	whimsical	sensitive
deceitful	modest	eccentric	maternal
vengeful	introverted	erratic	paternal
fiery	withdrawn	quick-witted	protective
volatile	affable	humorous	understanding
talkative	loquacious	jovial	serene
garrulous	benevolent	spontaneous	cautious
trustworthy	agreeable	mischievous	vivacious
reliable	malevolent	passionate	frivolous
dependable	extrovert	emotional	superficial
honest	rash	mean-spirited	gregarious
ruthless	demonstrative	imperious	philosophical
cruel	circumspect	arrogant	negligent
severe	ostentatious	overbearing	convivial
hostile	violent	condescending	irresponsible
self-possessed	tempestuous	unconventional	reckless
unassuming	threatening	supercilious	impudent
fickle	aggressive	scornful	derisive
genuine	vicious	disdainful	contemptuous
impertinent	hot-tempered	insolent	temerarious
intrepid	mercurial	ethical	irascible
honourable	audacious	reclusive	tolerant

CHARACTER FILE

Romeo

Act 1, Scene 1 – My Response	Key Adjectives
• emotional • sensitive • worried →	• honest • confused • upset • passionate • depressed • heart-broken
	Key Quotes

Romeo

Act 1, Scene 5 – My Response	Key Adjectives
	• sneaky
	• secretive
	• loving
	• inquisitive
	• confident
	• emotional
	• happy

	Key Quotes

CHARACTER FILE

Romeo

Act 2, Scene 2 – My Response	Key Adjectives
	o unsatisfied
	o unsure
	o romantic
	Key Quotes

Romeo

Act 2, Scene 4 – My Response	Key Adjectives
	Key Quotes

Romeo

Act 3, Scene 1 – My Response	Key Adjectives
	Key Quotes

Romeo

Act 3, Scene 3 – My Response	Key Adjectives
	Key Quotes

Romeo

Act 5, Scene 3 – My Response	Key Adjectives
	Key Quotes

Juliet

Act 1, Scene 3 – My Response	Key Adjectives
	• caring
	• shocked
	• obidient
	• happy
	• kind
	• polite
	• friendly
	• faithful
	• mannerly

	Key Quotes

Juliet

Act 1, Scene 5 – My Response	Key Adjectives
	○ happy
	○ friendly
	○ shocked
	○ caring
	○ loving
	○ kind
	Key Quotes

CHARACTER FILE

Juliet

Act 2, Scene 2 – My Response	Key Adjectives
	• happy
	• shocked
	• mannerly
	• loving
	• friendly
	• caring
	• honest
	Key Quotes

Juliet

Act 3, Scene 2 – My Response	Key Adjectives
	Key Quotes

CHARACTER FILE

Juliet

Act 3, Scene 5 – My Response	Key Adjectives
	Key Quotes

Juliet

Act 4, Scene 1 – My Response	Key Adjectives
	Key Quotes

CHARACTER FILE

Juliet

Act 4, Scene 3 – My Response	Key Adjectives
	Key Quotes

Tybalt

Scenes	Adjectives	My Response/Commentary

Benvolio

Scenes	Adjectives	My Response/Commentary

Benvolio

Scenes	Adjectives	My Response/Commentary

The Nurse

Scenes	Adjectives	My Response/Commentary
Scenes	Adjectives	My Response/Commentary

The Nurse

Scenes	Adjectives	My Response/Commentary

Friar Laurence

Scenes	Adjectives	My Response/Commentary
Scenes	Adjectives	My Response/Commentary

Friar Laurence

Scenes	Adjectives	My Response/Commentary

Mercutio

Scenes	Adjectives	My Response/Commentary

EXPLORING

Plot Structure

Pair Activity

Using **Freytag's Pyramid** as a guide, fill in the boxes below identifying the plot structure and main action that takes place at each stage of the play. For example, in the 'Exposition' box, you should mention that we are introduced to the characters, the setting and the action.

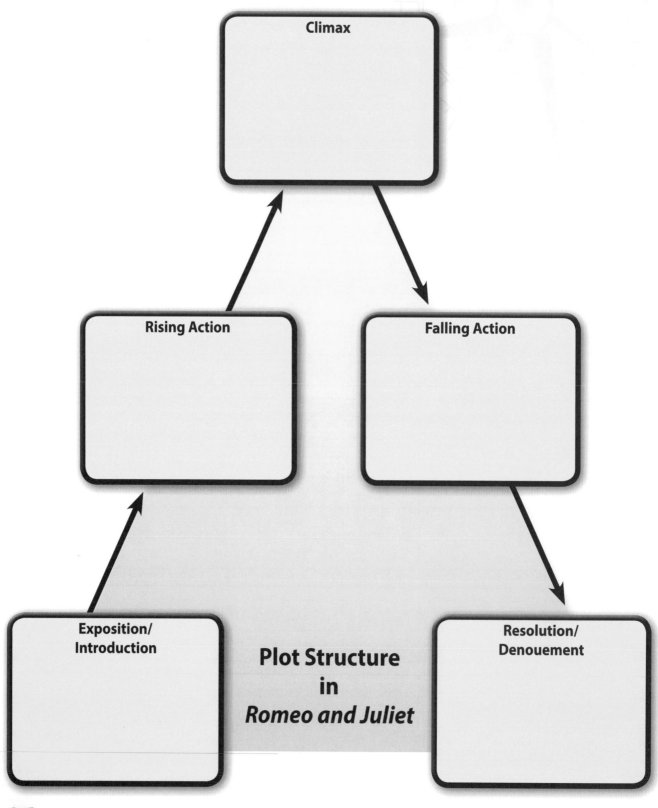

Climax

Rising Action

Falling Action

Exposition/ Introduction

Plot Structure in Romeo and Juliet

Resolution/ Denouement

Character Tracker

Choose your **favourite character** from the play, and using the diagram below as an example, track his/her development from start to finish on pages 106–107.

Place an **adjective** to describe this character on top of each 'step' in the diagram. Write the scene to which this adjective corresponds in the left column and include a quote or reference to support your adjective. Below is an example of a character tracker for Juliet.

Act 5, Scene 3	
Act 4, Scene 3	
Act 3, Scene 2	
Act 2, Scene 2	
Act 1, Scene 5	
Act 1, Scene 3	**Dutiful** • Juliet appears to be quite obedient as she discusses the prospect of marriage with her mother and the Nurse. • 'It is an honour that I dream not of.'

My Character Tracker for _____

Exploring an Important Character

Introduction (Relate to the question.)

The character of Juliet Capulet from *Romeo and Juliet* by William Shakespeare experiences many challenges and difficulties throughout the course of the play. Her relationship with Romeo Montague, the death of her cousin Tybalt, and being forced to marry Paris against her will are just three of the many challenges that Juliet faces in the play.

(a) Choose **three** out of the following five points to develop:

First Point

Topic sentence: **Juliet's relationship with Romeo causes her many problems in the play.**

Examples:

_____

_____

_____

_____

_____

_____

Discuss:

_____

_____

_____

_____

_____

_____

_____

Second Point

Topic sentence: The death of Juliet's cousin Tybalt, followed by Romeo's banishment, causes Juliet much grief and upset in the play.

Examples:

_____

_____

_____

_____

_____

Discuss:

_____

_____

_____

_____

_____

_____

Third Point

Topic sentence: Another challenge that Juliet faces is when her parents force her to marry Paris against her will.

Examples:

_____

_____

_____

_____

_____

Discuss:

_____

_____

_____

_____

_____

Fourth Point

Topic sentence: Juliet faces her greatest fears when she takes the potion that Friar Laurence has given her.

Examples:

_____

_____

_____

_____

_____

Discuss:

_____

_____

_____

_____

_____

Fifth Point

Topic sentence: The final challenge that Juliet faces is when she wakes early in the tomb and realises that Friar Laurence's plan has failed.

Examples:

_____

_____

_____

_____

_____

Discuss:

_____

_____

_____

_____

_____

At a Glance: Important Characters and their Scenes

ROMEO	JULIET	THE NURSE	FRIAR LAURENCE
Act 1, Scene 1	Act 1, Scene 3	Act 1, Scene 3	Act 2, Scene 3
Act 1, Scene 2	Act 1, Scene 5	Act 1, Scene 5	Act 2, Scene 6
Act 1, Scene 4	Act 2, Scene 2	Act 2, Scene 2	Act 3, Scene 3
Act 1, Scene 5	Act 2, Scene 5	Act 2, Scene 4	Act 4, Scene 1
Act 2, Scene 1	Act 2, Scene 6	Act 2, Scene 5	Act 4, Scene 5
Act 2, Scene 2	Act 3, Scene 2	Act 3, Scene 2	Act 5, Scene 2
Act 2, Scene 3	Act 3, Scene 5	Act 3, Scene 3	Act 5, Scene 3
Act 2, Scene 4	Act 4, Scene 1	Act 3, Scene 5	
Act 2, Scene 6	Act 4, Scene 2	Act 4, Scene 2	
Act 3, Scene 1	Act 4, Scene 3	Act 4, Scene 4	
Act 3, Scene 3	Act 4, Scene 5	Act 4, Scene 5	
Act 3, Scene 5	Act 5, Scene 3		
Act 5, Scene 1			
Act 5, Scene 3			

BENVOLIO	MERCUTIO	TYBALT	PARIS
Act 1, Scene 1	Act 1, Scene 4	Act 1, Scene 1	Act 1, Scene 2
Act 1, Scene 2	Act 2, Scene 1	Act 1, Scene 5	Act 3, Scene 4
Act 1, Scene 4	Act 2, Scene 4	Act 3, Scene 1	Act 4, Scene 1
Act 1, Scene 5	Act 3, Scene 1		Act 4, Scene 5
Act 2, Scene 1			Act 5, Scene 3
Act 2, Scene 4			
Act 3, Scene 1			

My *Romeo and Juliet* Glossary (Key Words)

Word	Meaning	Word	Meaning
Grievance	Problem		
An	If		
Wherefore	Why		
Art	Are		